Five Little Ducks

and other number rhymes

Illustrated by
Sharon Harmer

Miles Kelly

One Potato

One potato, two potato,
Three potato, four;
Five potato, six potato,
Seven potato more.

Hickety Pickety

Hickety pickety my black hen,
She lays eggs for gentlemen.
Sometimes nine and
sometimes ten,
Hickety pickety my black hen.

Hickory Dickory Dock

Hickory dickory dock,
The mouse ran up the clock,
The clock struck one,
The mouse ran down,
Hickory, dickory, dock.

Hickory dickory dock,
The mouse ran up the clock,
The clock struck two,
The mouse said, "Boo!"
Hickory dickory dock.

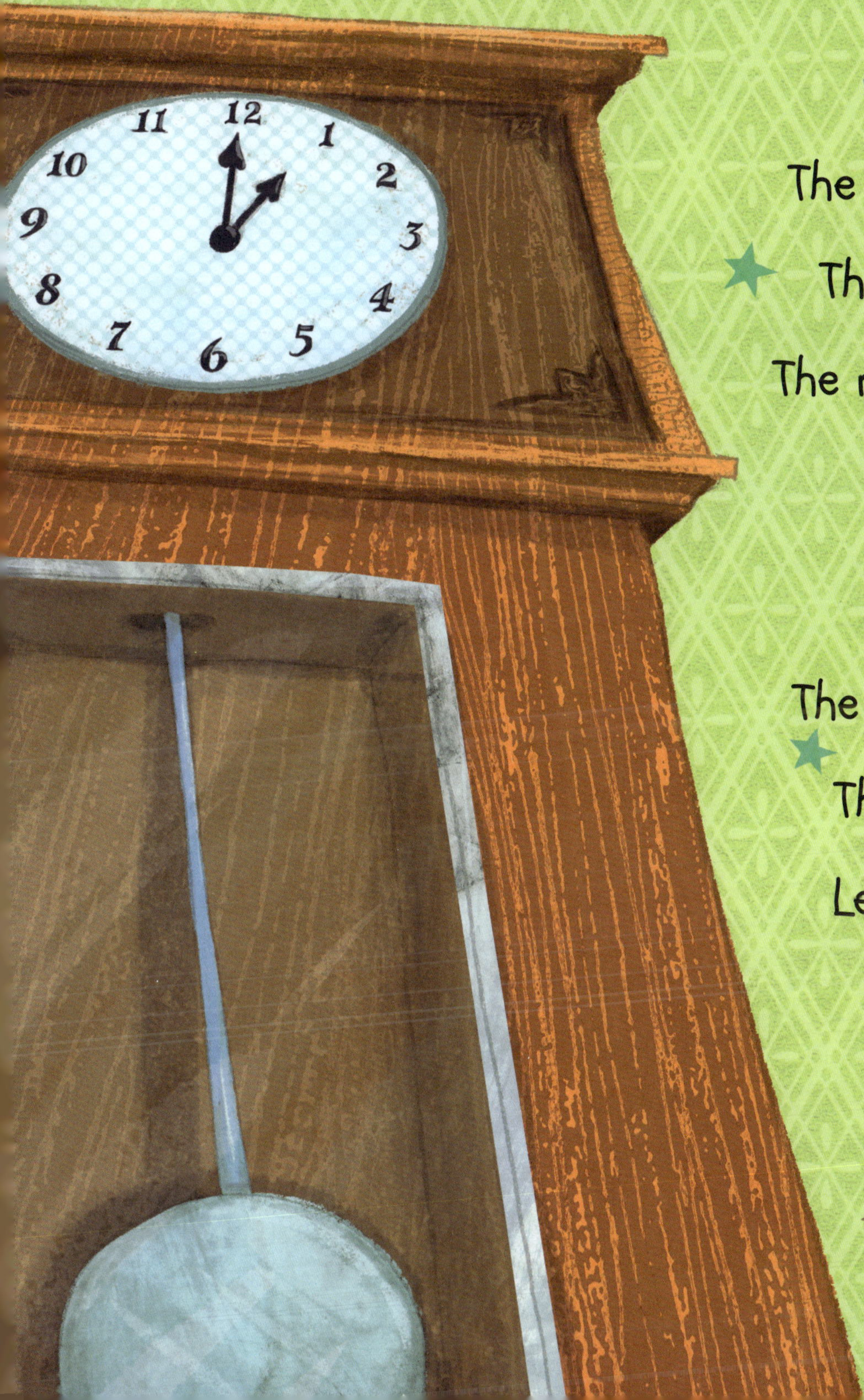

Hickory dickory dock,
The mouse ran up the clock,
The clock struck three,
The mouse said, "Weeee!"
Hickory dickory dock.

Hickory dickory dock,
The mouse ran up the clock,
The clock struck four,
Let's sing some more,
Hickory dickory dock.

Five Little Ducks

Five little ducks went
swimming one day,
Over the hill and far away.
Mother duck said, "Quack,
quack, quack, quack!"
And only four little ducks
came back.

Four little ducks went
swimming one day,
Over the hill and far away.
Mother duck said, "Quack,
quack, quack, quack!"
And only three little ducks
came back.

Three little ducks went
swimming one day,
Over the hill and far away.
Mother duck said, "Quack,
quack, quack, quack!"
And only two little ducks
came back.

Two little ducks went
swimming one day,
Over the hill and far away.
Mother duck said, "Quack,
quack, quack, quack!"
And only one little duck
came back.

One little duck went
swimming one day,
Over the hill and far away.
Mother duck said,
"Quack, quack,
quack, quack!"
And all her five little ducks
came back.

Rub-a-dub-dub

Rub-a-dub-dub,
Three men in a tub,
And who do you think they be?
The butcher, the baker,
The candlestick maker,
And all of them going to sea.

One, Two, Three, Four, Five

One, two, three, four, five,
Once I caught a fish alive.
Six, seven, eight, nine, ten,
Then I let it go again.

Why did you let it go?
Because it bit my finger so.
Which finger did it bite?
This little finger on my right.

Two Little Dicky Birds

Two little dicky birds sitting on a wall,
One named Peter, one named Paul.
Fly away Peter, fly away Paul,
Come back Peter, come back Paul!

One, Two, Buckle my Shoe

One, two,
buckle my shoe.

Three, four,
knock at the door.

Five, six, pick up sticks.

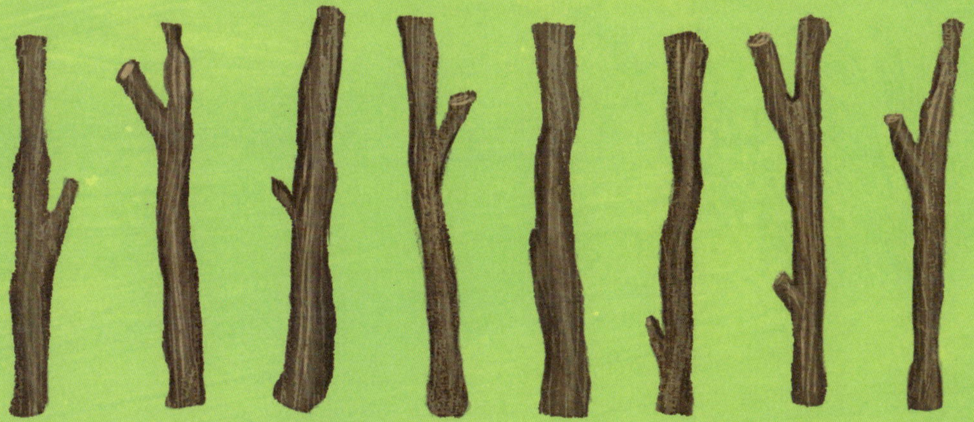

Seven, eight, lay them straight.

Nine, ten,
a good fat hen.

Five Little Pussy-cats

Five little pussy-cats
playing near the door,
One ran and hid inside
And then there were four.

Four little pussy-cats
underneath a tree,
One heard a dog bark
And then there were three.

Three little pussy-cats
thinking what to do,
One saw a little bird
And then there were two.

Two little pussy-cats
sitting in the sun,
One ran to catch his tail
And then there was one.

One little pussy-cat looking
for some fun,
He saw a butterfly
And then there were none.

One, Two, Three, Four

One, two, three, four,
Mary at the kitchen door.
Five, six, seven, eight,
Eating cherries off a plate.

Hot Cross Buns!

Hot cross buns! Hot cross buns!
One a penny, two a penny,
Hot cross buns!
Give them to your daughters,
Give them to your sons,
One a penny, two a penny,
Hot cross buns!

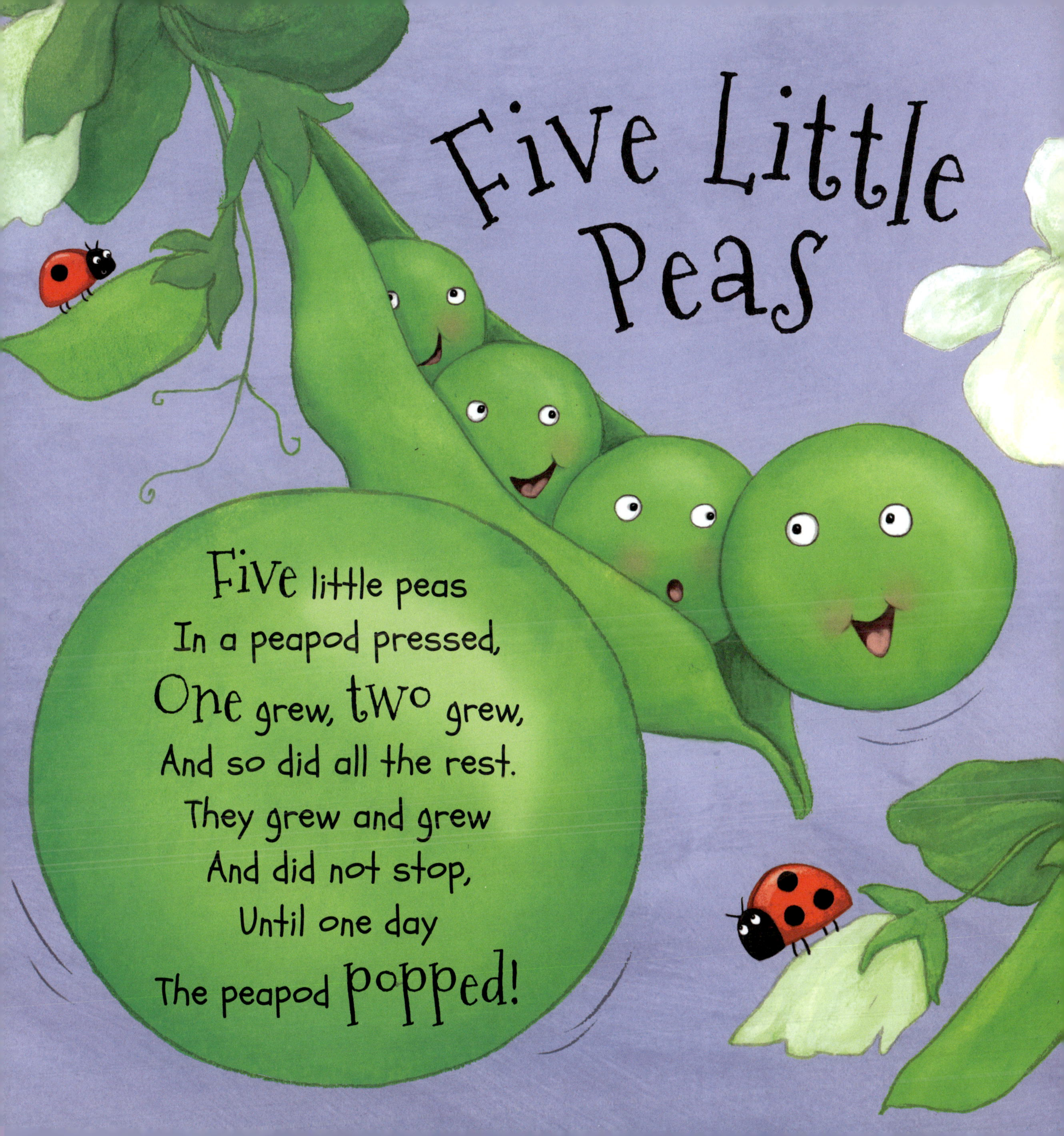

Five Little Peas

Five little peas
In a peapod pressed,
One grew, two grew,
And so did all the rest.
They grew and grew
And did not stop,
Until one day
The peapod popped!

I Saw Three Ships

I saw three ships
come sailing by,
Come sailing by,
Come sailing by,
I saw three ships
come sailing by,
On New Year's Day
in the morning.

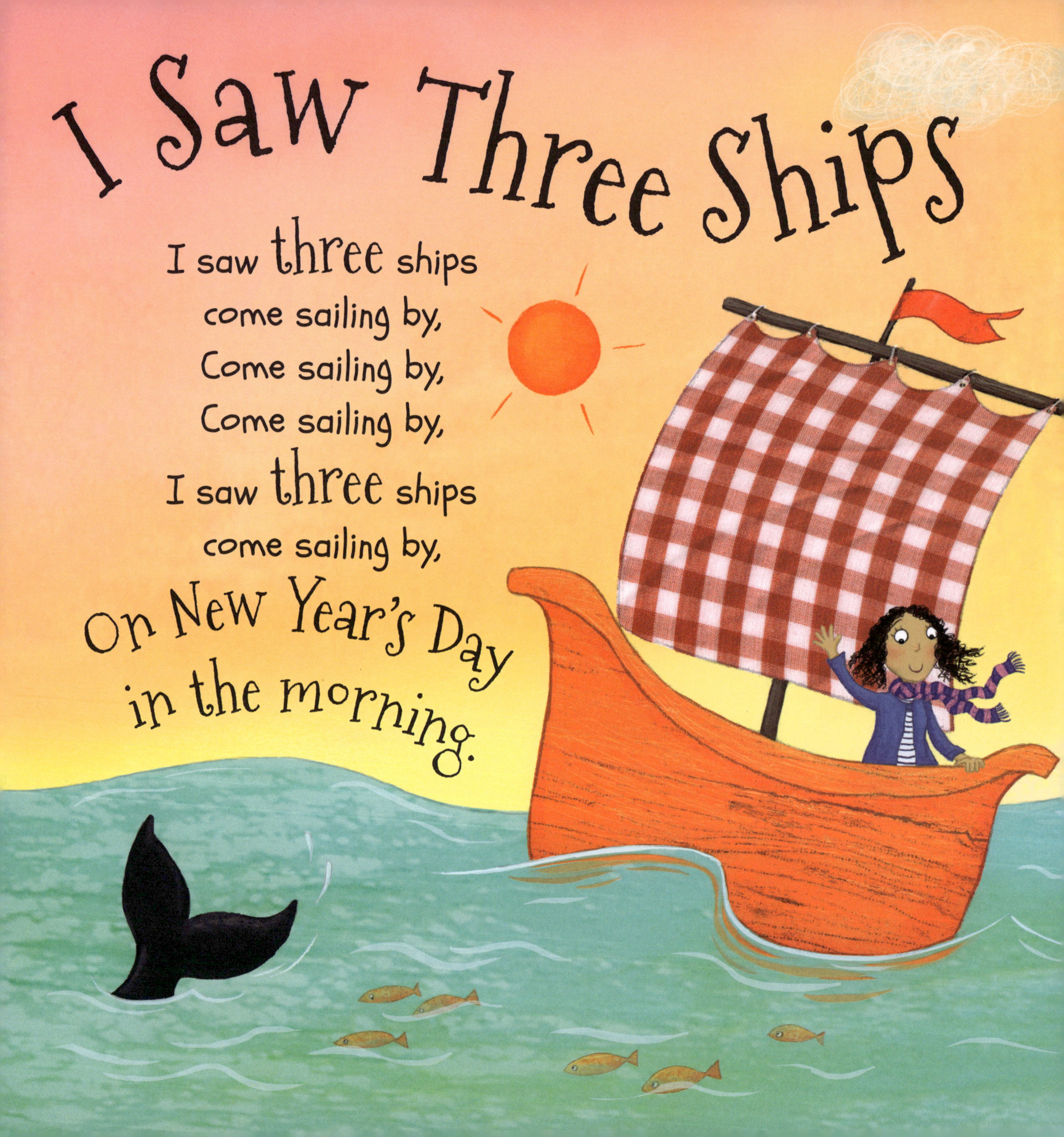

And what do you think was in them then,
Was in them then, was in them then?
And what do you think was in them then,

On New Year's Day in the morning?

Three pretty girls
were in them then,
Were in them then,
were in them then,
Three pretty girls
were in them then,
On New Year's Day in the morning.

One for Sorrow

One for sorrow,
Two for joy,
Three for a girl,
Four for a boy.
Five for silver,

Six for gold,
Seven for a secret,
Never to be told.
Eight for a wish,
Nine for a kiss,
Ten for a bird you want to miss.

The End